D1277376

George,
The Pavilion Cat

Brighton & Hove

GEORGE was a real cat who strayed into the Royal Pavilion in Brighton and stayed there for about twelve years, until he died in 1980.

He is buried in the Preston Manor Walled Garden. Buried with him was the special rug that was made for him while he was living at the Pavilion. A small headstone records his name.

The author and illustrator first met at Brighton Art College. A shared love of children, cats and Brighton led Judy Pennington and Julia Pannett-Sexton to bring George's story to a wider audience.

EVERY day, the black and white cat walked round the streets of Brighton.

One day be turned a corner and saw something quite magical.

It was the Royal Pavilion, shining in the sunlight. It looked just like a palace out of a fairy story, with its domes and minarets, and it was true that a Prince had built it long, long ago.

The cat had never seen anything like it.

There and then he decided that this was where he wanted to live.

E walked boldly through the big front door and miaowed loudly.

"No animals allowed in here!" said a gruff voice, and a large hand started to pick him up.

"Oh, just let him have a look around," said another, softer voice, and a gentle hand stroked him. "I wonder what his name is – he hasn't got a collar."

"You're too soft-hearted, Rosemary," said Gruff Voice.

The cat purred happily. He liked the beautiful furniture and carpets, and was determined to stay.

ROSEMARY gave him some food, and he fell asleep on one of the soft chairs.

When he woke up, it was very quiet. The Royal Pavilion had been locked up, and everyone had gone home.

He decided to explore.

The rooms were large and full of amazing things.

He came to an enormous dining room with a long table laid for a meal. The cat looked up and saw a glittering light made of hundreds of glass pieces. It was held up by a fierce dragon – not a real one of course!

E walked on until he came to a big kitchen. But there were no food smells. The kitchen had not been used for a long time. George licked his lips as he saw a chicken on a roasting spit in the fireplace, but it was not a real one – only a model – and no warm fire burned in the grate.

He jumped up on to one of the dressers where many shiny copper pans were hanging in long rows. He walked along the shelf and then stopped to clean his whiskers. When he looked up he got a fright – there was another black and white cat right by him! It was his reflection in the bottom of a plate.

He jumped down, and then had another surprise.

A big rat sat on the floor in the middle of the room. George crouched down, the rat did not move. George pounced. The rat fell over stiffly.

It was a stuffed rat. What a trick to play on a cat! George was cross. He did not like this kitchen.

E was allowed to stay in the Pavilion, and the people who looked after it named him George, after the Prince who had once lived there.

Rosemary was his special friend. Her job was to show visitors round the Pavilion every day and she always introduced them to George the cat.

She never forgot to bring him something tasty to eat, and he grew quite sleek and fat.

George was pleased with his new name and proud to be known as the Pavilion cat. He had a job as well, which was to keep the building free of mice. It was a wonderful life.

Visitors came from far-off countries and spoke in different languages. They stroked George, and used words he didn't understand.

What has George seen on the stairs?

GEORGE was the most fortunate cat in Brighton. He had the choice of so many sleeping places, and he slept most of the day.

One day he was curled up fast asleep on a nice warm patch of carpet when he felt a hard prod and woke up with a jolt.

"Don't poke George!" he heard Rosemary say. One of the visitors had jabbed him with his walking stick!

"I thought it was a stuffed cat!" said the man, laughing. George got up and walked away, waving his tail angrily. Then he remembered the stuffed rat in the kitchen – he had been fooled then!

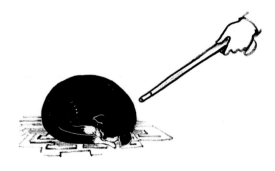

A film was going to be made at the Royal Pavilion, and everyone was talking about it, and looking forward to seeing famous film stars.

George thought he would like to be a film star. He had looked in one of the big mirrors and seen how handsome he was.

But when all the film people arrived he was a bit frightened of all the noise and bustle, the bright lights and the wires everywhere. Lots of people were walking about in strange old-fashioned clothes.

"Get that cat out of here!" shouted a man with a very loud voice.

George was outraged. He was not used to being shouted at. Didn't they know who he was? He hid under a settee, out of the way.

beautiful lady in a long dress picked him up and stroked him.

"What a lovely cat!" she said, as George purred in her arms. "He must be in the film – they did have pets in the old days. Please let him be in the story!"

The shouting man mopped his forehead and waved his arms. "I've got enough problems without having to cope with animals – get him off the set!"

The lady was disappointed, and put George down at the doorway. He walked off in a huff and gave himself a good wash. He knew he was a star already in his special home – why should he worry about a silly film?

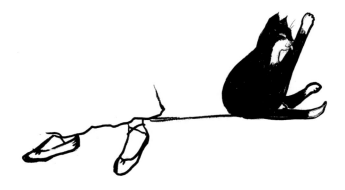

"THE Queen is coming to the Pavilion!" said Rosemary, one day. "We must make everywhere look really smart. There's such a lot to do!"

Everyone was very busy and did not have time to give George any attention, which made him a bit cross.

There was going to be a big dinner in the dining room, which they called the Banqueting Room. The long table was laid with shining dishes and tall candlesticks were placed on the white tablecloth.

This person must be very important, he thought, so of course she will want to meet me. So when the Queen arrived, he sat right in the middle of the doorway, and she could not get past.

Everyone looked at George.

Rosemary stepped forward. "This is George, the Pavilion cat, ma'am," she said.

A silk-gloved hand came down and stroked his head. George purred proudly.

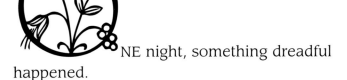NE night, something dreadful happened.

George was creeping around looking for mice, when he heard a strange noise. A crackling and hissing sound.

He wondered what it was. He sniffed the air and felt afraid, for he could smell a strong, burning smell.

He went to see what was happening and stopped near the Music Room.

IT WAS ON FIRE!

Glass was breaking and fierce flames were burning the heavy curtains. Pieces of ceiling were falling down.

George didn't know what to do. Something terrible was happening but how could he get help? His marvellous home was going to burn down.

LUCKILY, a night-watchman had also heard the noise and had called the Fire Brigade.

George ran away and hid under a bed all night.

The firemen were fighting to stop the fire spreading to the rest of the Pavilion. There were big puddles of water everywhere and black, choking smoke billowed out of the Music Room, which was now a shocking sight.

Rosemary came early in the morning and cried when she saw the mess. She found George and picked him up and held him tightly.

"Poor George, you must have been so frightened," she said, stroking him gently. "And this room has been ruined – it will never be the same again."

It took a long time to repair the Music Room, but clever workmen did restore it. Thanks to their skills it looked even more beautiful than before.

A man from a carpet-making firm arrived one day. He measured some of the floors carefully for new carpets.

George was curious to know what was going on. He weaved round the man's legs, and played with the tape measure, which looked like a long snake. The man tickled him under the chin.

"This is George, the Pavilion cat," said Rosemary when she brought the man a cup of tea.

"Hello, George, you're a fine fellow!", he said.

"George is an important part of the Pavilion," Rosemary told him.

"Then I have an idea," said the man, smiling. "He must have his very own rug!"

WHEN the new carpets arrived, there was a small parcel with them, addressed to George.

"This is your own special rug, George," said Rosemary, as she undid the string.

The little square rug had his name woven into the pattern. George was very pleased, especially when a newspaper reporter came with a photographer to take a picture of George sitting on his new rug.

But for sleeping on, the Royal beds were softer and cosier.

Sometimes, the visitors would see a little lump under a bedcover.

"That looks a lumpy bed!" one of them might say. "The beds must have been uncomfortable in the old days."

But *you* know what the lump was, don't you!

EORGE yawned and stretched as he sat on a soft chair in the hall. He watched the visitors come through the big front door and purred happily when they spoke to him and stroked him.

What a lucky day it had been when he had turned that corner and seen the Royal Pavilion shining in the sun.

He had found the best, the most special home in the whole town. ⌒

GEORGE
THE
PAVILION
CAT

1965 — 1980